Florence Nightingale

Betty Lou Kratoville

ORDER DIRECTLY FROM
ANN ARBOR PUBLISHERS LTD.
P.O. BOX 1, BELFORD
NORTHUMBERLAND NE70 7JX
TEL. 01668 214460 FAX 01668 214484
www.annarbor.co.uk

Cover Design: Nanette Brichetto
Cover Photo: Pictorial History Research
Interior Illustrations: Damon Rarey

International Standard Book Number: 1-57128-145-2

10 09 08 07 06 05 04 03
1   0   9 8 7 6 5 4 3

Contents

CHAPTER 1

The Goal

If you had lived during the 1800s, you would have been afraid to go to the hospital. You would have heard that more people died there than got well. They were dark and dirty places. A person with one disease might be jammed into bed with someone with quite a different disease. Nurses were not trained. Often they were found to be drunk on the job.

Army hospitals were even worse. There were few beds. The wounded lay on bare floors. No one answered their cries for water. There were no clean bandages. The food was poor. Men with minor wounds often died. No one seemed to care.

Florence Nightingale cared. It was she who first began the fine nursing care we expect today. And she had to fight to do it. She had to fight her family and friends. She had to fight the men who ruled England. In those days men would not listen to a young woman's ideas. No matter! Florence would not listen to them either.

Her family was on a trip to Italy when Florence was born. It seemed right to give her the name of the city of her birth. The Nightingales were a wealthy family. They had two houses in the country. Winters were spent in London. They liked to give parties. Their homes were often filled with guests of high rank.

Florence and her sister, Parthe, were taken on trips to Europe. On one great day they were presented to Queen Victoria. But this kind of life was not for Florence. She knew what she wanted. And it wasn't the pleasure-filled ways of her family.

She had been a thoughtful child. She liked to pretend that her dolls were hurt or in pain. Then she would nurse them back to health. When she grew older, she took care of sick aunts and cousins. Now and then she heard of someone ill in the village. She rushed to their bedside to see what she could do. This seemed to upset her family and friends.

Florence had only one wish. She wanted to be a nurse with all her heart. Nothing must stop her.

There were no nursing schools for women in England at that time. Yet there must be a way.

She wrote letter after letter to schools in other countries. Somewhere there had to be a place that would teach her what she wanted to know.

One day a friend told her about a hospital in Germany. It trained women students as nurses. Florence went there at once. It was just what she had been looking for. Quickly she went home to tell her parents.

"No," thundered her father. "You cannot go!"

"I don't understand," said her mother. "You have such a good life here."

Florence did not give up. She asked her sister to help her. But her sister agreed with their parents. "I don't understand you, Florence," she said. "Why would you want to go to a place where there's blood and pain and death?"

Then Florence knew she would get no help from Parthe. But she did not give up. It took her a whole year. But at last her parents gave in.

"But you cannot tell anyone where you are," her father said. "We will say that you have gone away for your health."

Florence didn't care. She was on her way!

Life at the German hospital was hard. Students rose at 5:00 A.M. They scrubbed floors. They changed sheets. They bathed the sick. Their plain meals lasted only 10 minutes. But life had meaning for Florence at last!

CHAPTER 2

The Next Step

Florence learned a lot in her months at the German hospital. But she knew she had much more to learn. Once again she would have to leave England. Once again her family tried to stop her.

Her sister would not get out of bed. "I am ill," she groaned to Florence. "You cannot leave me."

Her parents were not much better. They would not listen to her plans. Florence stood it as long as she could. Then she packed her bags and left for Paris.

What a change! In Paris all doors were open to her. She toured hospitals and clinics. She walked through wards with doctors. They even let her watch them operate. Florence didn't miss a thing. She took notes. She made lists. She asked lots of questions. She became expert in the field of nursing.

What to do with all this training? How to put all she had learned to work? And then she heard about the perfect job. A new hospital for poor women had been built in London. It was to open in ten days. Fine! But who would run it? Who would buy all the supplies? Who would get the hospital ready for patients to move into?

Then someone thought of Florence Nightingale. The job was just right for her, and she knew it. She did not waste any time. The men who hired her stood back in wonder. How could one woman know so much? How could one woman *do* so much?

Florence got rid of worn sheets and dirty pillows and furniture. She bought dozens of new brooms and mops. And she made sure they were used. She worked as hard as her staff – or harder. Some of them loved her. Others quit. Florence paid no attention. She just kept on caring for the poor and the sick.

In 1854 cholera swept through London. The

She worked as hard as her staff.

hospital beds quickly filled up. Now Florence had a new problem. She couldn't find enough good nurses. Then she had an idea. She wrote to farmers all over England.

"Send me your daughters," her letter said. "I will train them to be good nurses. Then they will always have work."

The farmers sent their daughters. Florence trained them. Slowly nursing began to turn into work that was well thought of.

Florence was head of the hospital. Yet no job was too lowly for her. She held dying cholera victims in her arms. She carried trays. She changed sheets. She swept and mopped and scrubbed. She used her own money to send people to the seaside. There the air was fresh and clean. They could get well faster. No job was too great or too small.

Florence did not know it but she was getting ready for a huge job that lay ahead.

CHAPTER 3

The War

In 1854 Turkey was at war with Russia. England and France agreed to help Turkey. So the English army was sent to the Crimea where the war was being fought. The English people were proud of their army. They thought it the best in the world. They cheered as the troops marched off to war. Bands played. Flags waved.

The brave English troops were doomed to defeat. Not by their Russian enemies. But by disease and filth. By lack of good food and good care. Some men died in battle. Many more died of neglect.

Thirty thousand men were shipped across the Black Sea. Plans for this action had been poor. There was little food on board the ships. There was not enough water. Cholera broke out. The weak men fought bravely. They forced the Russians to retreat.

Now something had to be done for the wounded. They were put on ships. Another awful trip back across the Black Sea to Scutari. Horror awaited them there. There was just one hospital. It was already full of men with cholera. An old dirty barracks was turned into a hospital. It was an awful place. There were no beds. There were no cups to hold a sip of water for the suffering men. There were no tables, no chairs, few doctors. Men wrapped in bloody blankets lay on the floor. And, hard to believe, there were no nurses!

Tales of of the plight of these poor men reached England. The English people were shocked. This could not be happening to the troops who had left England with high hopes and brave hearts. Something had to be done. Once again someone thought of Florence Nightingale.

"Would you be willing to go to the Crimea?" she was asked. "And to take a group of nurses with you?"

"I will go," she agreed. "What about

supplies?"

"Oh, don't worry. Everything you need is there," came the answer.

Better be safe than sorry, thought Florence. And she went to work. She filled boxes and boxes. Some held clean linens. Some held medicine and bandages. She found some barrels and packed them to the brim with food.

After a long hard trip Florence and her 38 nurses got to Scutari. She had been warned about what she might find there. Even so, she was shocked by the Barracks Hospital. There were *four miles* of men lying in filth. Rats and fleas were everywhere. The kitchen, if one could call it that, was a mess. Few pans or kettles. Tea and meat were boiled in the same unwashed pots. Tables were full of dirty dishes and spoiled food. The nurses did not even have lamps or candles to light their own rooms.

At first the doctors were not pleased to have Florence there. She and her nurses had to be careful not to offend them. But at last the huge tide of wounded men changed the doctors' minds. It was clear that they had to have help even if they didn't want it. Florence and her team were free to pitch in. And pitch in they did!

The men's clothes had not been washed in five weeks. The nurses boiled the clothes. They scrubbed the men. They threw away matresses that were full of fleas. They made new ones of clean straw. They cooked vats of good hot soup.

Florence had been wise to bring her own supplies. They were soon gone. She wrote an angry letter to London. "We need everything. And we need it *fast*." Soon crates of soap, trays, dishes, sheets, and other items came. Now men lived instead of died.

A new problem came up. Wounded men still poured in. There was not another inch of space for more beds. Earlier one wing of the hospital had burned. It could not be used. No one did anything about it. What a waste, thought Florence. She dipped into her own money. The wing was fixed.

The men tried not to complain. But they

She was known as "the Lady with a Lamp."

were homesick and afraid. Florence tried to cheer them. At night she moved among them. A lamp lighted her way along the miles of beds. From then on she was known as the "Lady with a Lamp."

CHAPTER 4

Scutari Winter

The winter was hard and long in the Crimea. Sleet, snow, and mud kept armies at a standstill. The worst enemy was sickness. The soldiers were not well-fed. Their tents were wet and freezing. They were not given warm clothes. Thousands grew sick with fever, coughs, flu, and worse. "Send them to Miss Nightingale," barked their leaders.

And so they came – and came – and came. Florence took them in no matter how short of space she was. Yet she felt that something was very, very wrong. These were English soldiers. But their clothes were thin and worn. She could tell from their hollow eyes that they were half-starved. Many came with painful frostbite. No wonder it took so long for them to get better. When well, they were sent back to duty. And, of course, it wasn't long before they were sick again.

The army hospitals' way to fix a meal was strange. Each day the rations for one man was put in a small cloth bag. Then the hundreds of bags were dumped into a huge pot of boiling water. Of course, the food was not fit to eat. And the men grew thinner and thinner. Florence stopped this

22

practice as soon as she could. Not only at the Barracks Hospital but at all the hospitals in the war zone.

Florence did not only tend to the men's health. She worried about their minds. They needed something to do with their free time. She knew they drank a lot. And why not? They had nothing else to do in the cold, dark months. She set up a reading room. The men flocked to it.

The reading room was such a hit, Florence began a classroom. First one, then another. She stocked them with books, games, music, and maps. People in England heard about her latest idea. They sent money and, best of all, two teachers to hold classes.

Now the men were not spending their pay on drink. Florence had another thought. Should they not send some of their pay home? She wrote to Queen Victoria about this. The Queen said yes! So Florence began a Money Order Office. Soon wives and children were getting funds from their men at the front. It helped them a lot. Word spread. Within six months money order offices were opened all over the Crimea.

Florence felt good about her work. She said, "I have never seen so helpful a group as the English soldiers. Give them a chance to send money home, and they will use it. Give them schools, and they will come to them. Give them books and games, and they will leave off drinking. Give them suffering, and they will bear it. Give them work, and they will do it."

At last the long hours and worry caught up with Florence. She came down with a high fever. For two weeks she lay near death. Although she slowly got better, she was never strong again.

Perhaps it was time to go home. But she would never forget the brave soldiers and the lives she and her hard-working nurses had saved.

CHAPTER 5

Homecoming

The war in the Crimea was over. The fighting was at an end at last. It took months before the last soldiers left the hospital. Then and only then did Florence feel that she, too, could go home.

She heard that a huge welcome was planned for her. There would be thousands of people. There would be dozens of speeches. There would be bands and flags and flowers. Oh, no, thought Florence. Somehow she slipped into England secretly. She went first to a convent she knew to pray and to rest. Then she went straight to her home in the country. She had hoped life would be quiet there. She was wrong!

She got a ton of mail. Most letters just told her what a fine job she had done. But others asked for money or jobs. Some even asked for her hand in marriage! Newspapers begged for interviews. She was asked to give speeches. Florence kept on saying no.

For a while she thought her work was finished. She was wrong. And as time passed she knew it. What she did not know was that 40 years of hard work lay ahead.

What to do first? Well, why not take on the English army? Florence still had nightmares about the Barracks Hospital in the Crimea. And she knew that all army hospitals were much the same.

Help came from Queen Victoria. The queen asked Florence to come to the palace. She and her husband, Prince Albert, listened to all Florence had to tell them. They asked her to come back again and again. It was a good start.

Florence wanted to visit army hospitals all over England. The hospital heads did not want her there. But they dared not say so. It was clear that Florence had Queen Victoria on her side.

As she toured, Florence saw things that shocked her. Not only the hospitals were damp and filthy. So were the barracks in which the men lived. The food in peacetime was just as bad as it had been during the war years. At least 1,500 young soldiers died each year of poor food and disease.

"Our soldiers," Florence said, "join our army and die in barracks not in war!"

All this she put in a report. It took her six months to write it. It was 1,000 pages long. Important men read the report. They fought her ideas of reform. But the public was on her side. And that helped. The more these men tried to defeat her plans for change, the more the people upheld her views.

At last change came. It was slow but it was steady. Barracks were rebuilt. Hospitals were cleaned up. In three years the death rate of soldiers in England was cut in half. Florence Nightingale with very little help had brought health and comfort and life to the men of the English army.

CHAPTER 6

The Nurses

What next? Florence looked around for something else to fix. She didn't have to look far. She had seen a lot in her tours of army hospitals. She knew that nurses were not well-trained. And she knew there were too few of them. So she sat down and wrote a small book. It was called *Notes on Nursing: What it is and what it is not.* It was read all over England. People in other lands read it, too. Its message was simple and clear: cleanliness in all things.

Then she thought of the Nightingale Fund. It had been started to buy a gift for the "lady with the lamp." But Florence had turned down the gift. "Keep the money," she said. "One day it will fill a great need."

What great need was there? A training school for nurses! The Nightingale Fund had grown large. Florence was able to open her school. The plan for the school was very plain: Train nurses to train nurses! In this way hospitals would have the nursing staffs they so badly needed.

It was never easy. At that time doctors did not agree with Florence. Special training for nurses? Nonsense! They could learn all they needed to know just by watching doctors. Florence went right ahead with her plans. She chose St. Thomas Hospital in London for her school. Word about it spread. Soon the school was full.

Her students were carefully picked. They had to bring letters from home. The letters said they were honest girls from good families. Each student wore a plain uniform. Each student had her own room. Rules were strict. Class work was hard. Young women came from all over England.

Florence did not teach at the school. But she knew what went on there. She was always kind to her students. She knew how hard their nursing jobs would be.

In just a year or two the school had become famous. Florence heard from hospitals all over the world. They wanted to hire her nurses to start new schools to train more nurses. Why not? thought Florence. She sent nurses to Australia, Canada, Sweden, and other lands.

About this time she heard from America. A Civil War had begun there. President Lincoln wanted help. He knew that hospitals had to be well-run during a war. Florence was glad to lend a hand.

Never strong, she was working day and night. Once again she became very ill. By Christmas Eve 1861 she was close to death. But a few weeks later she was able to sit up in bed. She could not walk and was carried from room to room.

She wrote her letters, books, and reports from her bed. She liked to have her three cats nearby. Now and then a letter would bear a pawprint from one of the cats. Illness did not slow her down. There was still so much work to be done.

CHAPTER 7

India!

England ruled over India for years. The English tried to do a good job there. They built railroads. They started schools. They taught farmers how to grow better crops. They worked hard to get rid of the hunger in the land.

Many Indians liked the English. They worked and played together. But then there were others. They felt the English should go home. They wished to rule themselves. These people made trouble whenever they could. Lots of

She wrote strong angry letters and reports.

trouble. The answer? A large English army in India at all times. And this is where Florence Nightingale played a part.

One day someone told her about India. They spoke of the army's poor health. They told her the death rate was very high. Why so many deaths? Bad water, poor food, dirty, crowded tents and barracks. The hospitals were even worse.

This is all Florence had to hear. She reached for her pen. She wrote strong, angry letters and reports. One report was called "How People May Live and Die in India." It told about the terrible lives soldiers were leading. Not only English soldiers. Indian troops, too.

Nothing happened. Her letters and reports

were tossed aside unread. Florence kept on writing. She wrote to men in England. She wrote to men in India. For five years she wrote. But the leaders in England and India had more important things on their minds. Or so they thought.

At last just a bit of change. A new Department of Health was set up in India. Things got a bit better. Another death rate was cut in half. That alone should have filled Florence with joy. But then the friend in India who had helped her most died. All new plans were dropped. The men who still had power knew that Florence was growing old. They knew she was not well. They no longer feared her and her pen.

Now Florence felt that she had failed. Five

years of hard work had not changed much in India. She wrote in her diary, "Oh, that I could do something for India!" Of course, she *had* done something. But in her mind not enough. Never enough.

CHAPTER 8

The Final Years

For the last 50 years of her life Florence was in poor health. No one knew quite what was wrong. It is thought she may never have got over the Crimean fever.

Florence stayed at home. She often did not leave her bed for days. She saw few visitors. She seemed to want to save her strength. Sick or well, there was still much work to be done.

The plight of the poor still troubled her. At that time England had a depressing workhouse in most towns. Here the poor were sent. Children without parents had to go to workhouses. Widows without funds spent their last days there. Men too old or too ill to work landed in the workhouse.

They were grim places. As bad as – if not worse than – prisons. The insane were kept with the sane. Smallpox swept through the workhouses. People grew sick and died. Their bodies were tossed into unmarked graves. No one did a thing about it. It was a nightmare that hung over the poor of England.

One poor man died from filth and gross neglect. The newspapers told his story. Florence read about it. It made her angry. She raged at the country's leaders. Once again months went by. No action. Her letters grew longer and angrier. At last her nurses were allowed into one workhouse. It was to be a test. For the first time poor people were cared for by a trained staff. The test was a success.

Now Florence pressed for a new law. It was very simple. One place for orphans. One place for the insane. Another place for the sick. No more workhouses! The law passed. Florence said, "This is a beginning. We shall get more in time."

She worked until her eyesight failed. Then friends read her mail to her. People still wrote for help. People still sent gifts and awards. In 1908 England gave her the Order of Merit. It is England's highest honor. Never before had it been given to a woman. "Too kind," Florence said faintly. "Too kind."

Two years later she quietly slipped away from life in her sleep.